THE SAVANNAH SIPPING SOCIETY

BY JONES HOPE WOOTEN

MUSIC AND THIRD-PARTY MATERIALS USE NOTE

IMPORTANT BILLING AND CREDIT REQUIREMENTS

ON LICENSING *THE SAVANNAH SIPPING SOCIETY*

We write strong female characters that are to be played by females. Under no circumstances should any role in this comedy be played by a male.

Nothing in the licenses for *The Savannah Sipping Society* (or any of the plays written by Jones Hope Wooten) gives the right to film video or audio record a performance, a rehearsal, or any part thereof. Placing any excerpts on YouTube, Facebook, or social media of any kind is a violation of copyright laws.

All of the characters portrayed in *The Savannah Sipping Society* are fictional creations, and any resemblance to real persons, living or dead, is purely coincidental.

AUTHORS' NOTE

We suggest up-tempo music be played pre- and post-show and at intermission. In the stage directions, we suggest specific styles of music for scene transitions, just enough to establish the mood.

We urge that scene changes be made as quickly as possible to maintain a lively pace for the play. In each act, it is important that each scene flows directly into the next. To accomplish this, we have provided sufficient time for the actors to clear props and make rapid costume changes. Stagehands should only be on the set at intermission and during the transition from Act One, Scene 1 to Scene 2, to quickly remove the bistro table and chairs.

Each monologue should be delivered facing the audience but without any interaction whatsoever with the audience during any monologue.

No dialogue should be provided for the non-speaking character in Act One, Scene 4.

The pronunciation of the last name of the character Marlafaye Mosley is "Moze-lee."

THE SAVANNAH SIPPING SOCIETY received its world premiere at Gypsy Theatre Company in the Sylvia Beard Theatre in Buford, Georgia, on February 11, 2016. It was directed by Mercury, who also was the technical director and sound and set designer. The stage manager was Alessa Walle; the production designer was Danielle Gustaveson, who was also the scenic, costume, and property designer; the lighting designer was Joel Coady; the lighting operator was Chelsea Martin; the sound engineer was John LaFontaine; the stage-hands were Dustin C. Burrell and Rachael Endrizzi; and the original Jones Hope Wooten show logo was designed by Jason Jeffers. The cast was as follows:

RANDA COVINGTON .... Eileen Koteles
MARLAFAYE MOSLEY .... Judith Beasley
DOT HAIGLER .... Bobbie Elzey
JINX JENKINS .... Lory Cox

Danielle Gustaveson appeared in the cameo role at the beginning of Act One, Scene 4.

CHARACTERS
(in order of appearance)

RANDA COVINGTON, 49

DOT HAIGLER, 69

MARLAFAYE MOSLEY, 57

JINX JENKINS, 53

And a non-speaking role at the beginning of Act One, Scene 4

PLACE

The second-story verandah of a Savannah home.
Other locations are suggested by lighting.

TIME

The present.

ACT ONE

Scene 1: Late morning, lobby/juice bar of a yoga studio.
Scene 2: A few days later, late afternoon, verandah of Randa's home.
              Hours later, the verandah.
Scene 3: One month later, late night, the verandah.
Scene 4: One week later, late afternoon, the verandah.

ACT TWO

Scene 1: Weeks later, late afternoon, the verandah.
Scene 2: Valentine's Day, late afternoon, the verandah.
              Later that night, the verandah.
Scene 3: Six weeks later, the verandah.
Scene 4: One month later, a hotel balcony.

THE SAVANNAH SIPPING SOCIETY

ACT ONE

Scene 1

Late morning. Up-tempo jazz plays as a pin spotlight comes up downstage right on Randa Covington, high-strung perfectionist, in trendy form-fitting yoga pants and off-one-shoulder top. Hair stylishly pulled back, a rolled mat under one arm, water bottle in hand, she faces the audience and speaks.

RANDA. *(Exudes confidence, upbeat.)* It's my firm belief — and certainly any clear-thinking individual would agree — that one must approach life from a *logical* point of view. It's my mantra. For example, any time I'm asked to fill out a form that includes the phrase "in case of a medical emergency please contact — " I always write … "*a doctor.*" Logic! It's how I built my successful career in architecture — working twenty-four-seven and accepting nothing less than perfection from myself. So, when a new partner was to be named at McCarthy & Fowler, it was *logical* my unflinching loyalty to the firm was about to be repaid. I was so proud as I walked into that conference room. *(Beat. Then, uncomfortable.)* You know, I don't actually *remember* screaming obscenities as the security guards pried my hands from the throat of the thirty-year-old *man* who *was* given the partnership. But when McCarthy & Fowler filed the restraining order against me, I completely understood because … it was *logical. (Shakes it off, determinedly upbeat.)* Anyway, having an excess of time to fill, logic dictates that I do something other than sit at home alone rearranging my sweaters according to cashmere content. And I may have stumbled on to a masterful way to heal body and spirit — yoga! *(Gets into it, indicates her costume.)* Obviously I have prepared and I am ready for the adventure. *This* will be wonderful! *(Her pin spotlight goes to black as another pin spotlight comes up downstage left on the lobby/juice bar in a yoga studio — bistro table, three chairs. "Spa"/new-age music plays softly in the background. Dot Haigler, daffy and endearing, in glasses, colorful exercise pants and top, is seated in a chair, fans herself vigorously. Randa, gasping, exhausted, joins her from stage right.)* That was the most horrible thing I've ever been through! Forcing otherwise sane women to squat and contort themselves in a small room, then cranking the heat to a hundred fifty degrees?! *Really?!* What homicidal maniac thought *that* up?! *(To Dot.)* Excuse me, mind if I collapse in this chair?

DOT. Please do! You certainly lasted longer than I did. I thought "*hot* yoga" meant it was fun and hip. Who knew we signed up for Lucifer's little sweatshop?

RANDA. *(Laughs.)* I guess what counts is that we tried.

DOT. I agree. Honestly, I'm at the age where all I usually exercise is *caution. (Extends her hand.)* I'm Dot.

RANDA. I'm Randa. Good to know at least *two* of us were smart enough to get out of there alive. *(They shake as Marlafaye Mosley, earthy, boisterous, good ol' Texas gal, in baggy sweatpants, sweatshirt with sleeves cut out, staggers in stage left, near collapse, drags a gym bag behind her.)*

MARLAFAYE. The pearly gates — they're openin' up! *(Croaks.)* Must … have … water! *(The others are alarmed. She sinks to her knees at the table.)*

RANDA. Oh! Okay, I'll go get — *(Marlafaye grabs Randa's bottle, chugs all of it, slams it back on the table.)* Or … just … help yourself to mine.

MARLAFAYE. Thank god I didn't slather on the baby oil this morning. I would've come out of that hellhole chicken fried. *(Indicates Dot's fan.)* Hey, could I get a little bit of that action?

DOT. Sure. At least this way I'll burn a *few* calories. *(Fans Marlafaye, who basks in the breeze.)* So, I take it you don't work out that much, either?

MARLAFAYE. Please. If it weren't for mood swings, I'd get no exercise at all. But that's okay, 'cause it just wouldn't be fair to the women of Savannah if I was *this* gorgeous, smart, funny, *and* thin. It's a public service, really.

DOT. How very thoughtful. *(Fans.)* Gee, what a waste of a perfectly good morning. I drove in all the way from Tybee Island to get here.

RANDA. That's the only positive part for me. I just had to walk from the end of the block. Mine's the butter yellow house covered with jasmine.
MARLAFAYE. Nice digs. *(Wipes her forehead.)* Boy howdy! I'm sweatin' like a hooker at altar call. I swear I've got a towel in here somewhere. *(Plops gym bag on table, rummages in it.)* By the way, I'm Marlafaye.
RANDA. I'm Randa. Randa Covington.
DOT. Dot Haigler. I was named for my great-aunt Rebecca. *(Off their looks.)* Oh, she had a huge mole in the middle of her forehead. We always called her Aunt Dot. *(Marlafaye pulls out various items from the bag, including a two-foot terrycloth rag doll. Dot picks it up.)* Oh, my. And who's *this* little fellow?
MARLAFAYE. *(Glances up, slightly embarrassed, takes it back.)* Don't think I always traipse around with a big ol' doll. I've been *encouraged* to keep it handy. It's what they call a mobile therapy device.
DOT. Oh. That's what my late husband used to call his whiskey flask.
MARLAFAYE. My ex's divorce lawyer forced me to take anger management classes. Turns out Mr. Happy Pants failed to see the humor in me cuttin' the crotch out of every pair of his Levis.
RANDA. Going out on a limb here, I take it your husband cheated on you?
MARLAFAYE. *(Anger slowly rises.)* Yeah. With a twenty-three-year-old dental hygienist. Now every time I brush my teeth, I think of them sneakin' around, livin' the high life, while I was bustin' my hump on the job and wonderin' what was wrong with my marriage! *(Loses it, beats the doll against the table. Louder.)* I should've known Waylon was tomcattin' when he started flossin' between meals! That's just not normal! *(Stops. Pants. Smiles, relaxed.)* Whew! *(Offers it to Dot.)* Got any man problems you'd like to get over?
DOT. Me? *(Takes it.)* Oh, no. Ross and I had a wonderful marriage. He passed away suddenly eight months ago just after we moved here. We always planned for a golden retirement, to live near the water, make new friends. But Ross kept putting it off. We did finally get here, but — *(Determinedly upbeat.)* No. I don't have any man problems, but thanks. *(Puts the doll on the table.)*
MARLAFAYE. How about you, Randa? Want to take a shot? It's the least I can do to thank you for the water. *(Unseen by them, Dot studies the doll with increasing interest, picks it up, starts to shake and choke it. Her vigor builds.)*

RANDA. Oh, no. Men haven't been in the picture for years. I'm a dyed-in-the-wool career gal, devoted my whole life to it. No, I don't have a — *(They notice Dot.)*

DOT. *(Fiery.)* I told you we were waiting too long! You wasted the best years of our lives. Now you've left me all alone in a strange city with a drawer full of sexy underwear that's absolutely useless to me! A woman has needs! *(Slaps the doll repeatedly.)*

MARLAFAYE. *(Gently pulls doll away.)* Whoa. Kinda early in the day for that much information, Dottie. You okay?

DOT. *(Refreshed.)* You know, you're right. That little doll's a real winner. Oh, come on, Randa. Take a crack at it. Feels great!

RANDA. Oh, no, I haven't been involved in a relationship for years. I'm sure there's no *therapy device* for my particular situation. It's career-related. You see, I was recently the victim of a vicious corporate downsizing.

MARLAFAYE. I am so sorry. How many employees did they fire?

RANDA. *(Confident façade shatters. Sobs.)* One! *(Wails.)* They gave my job to a thirty-year-old twit. He wears bow ties! *(Grabs doll, screams as she smashes its head repeatedly against the table.)*

MARLAFAYE. Hey, now! Easy, girl! That doll's got to last me another couple months. *(Marlafaye pulls the doll away.)*

RANDA. *(Calms down.)* I … don't know where that came from, but I feel much better now. I'm fine. *(Beat. Grabs the doll, gives it another whack, Marlafaye snatches it from her.)* Okay, *now* I'm fine.

MARLAFAYE. Wow! We may have bombed out of hot yoga but we sure let off some steam here today, right, girls? *(Shoves the doll into her bag.)*

DOT. I say good for us! And I don't think we bombed out here at all. Maybe we were meant to meet each other.

RANDA. Yes, maybe. It's ironic because I always avoid places like this. I'm starting to think the only way I'll ever expand my social horizon is to hire a life coach or find a miracle worker.

MARLAFAYE. Well, you won't catch *me* here again. I'm done with this exercise bull. I only joined this stupid class because my ex-husband bragged about how he and his trophy wife go to the gym and how he's lost fifty pounds since our divorce. He asked if I know what his ideal weight is and I said, "Sure. Four pounds *includin'* the urn." *(They laugh. She checks her watch.)* Gotta go. It was great to meet y'all.

RANDA. Yes, it *really* was. Another fifteen minutes and I would've invited you both over for drinks at my place. *(Laughs.)*

MARLAFAYE. Sounds great! Happy hour, six o'clock Friday night.
DOT. I'm in! *(To Randa.)* You get the wine, we'll bring the nibblies. *(She and Marlafaye exit stage left.)*
RANDA. *(Completely blindsided.)* What?! But we don't really …uh … okay … *(Tries to get into it. Calls.)* Great! The more the merrier! *(Light crossfades to black as downstage right pin spotlight comes up. Randa crosses into it, faces audience.)* Um … when I was thinking about widening my horizons I didn't *exactly* see the process beginning with me chatting up two sweaty escapees from a New Age death trap. But … maybe Dot's right. Maybe we *were* meant to meet each other. Of course Dot's a bit more mature and Marlafaye is … well, she's *definitely* the person I'd want on my side if I were to find myself, say, in a *bar fight*. But I have to wonder if the three of us have anything in common. Now I'm questioning why I agreed to get together with them again. Frankly, I'm just not seeing the *logic* in it. But, maybe that's part of opening myself to new experiences, like … *hot yoga. (Beat. Then, horrified.)* Oh god, what have I done? *(Blackout.)*

Scene 2

A few days later, late afternoon. Up-tempo country swing plays for only a few bars. Downstage left pin spotlight comes up on Marlafaye, now dressed in casual pants and shirt, carries an oversized purse.

MARLAFAYE. Know how you get that tingly feeling when you're fallin' in love? That sensation that washes over you and kinda gives you the shivers? Well, *that* is common sense leavin' your body. That's what happened to me on that black day I met Waylon Mosley. Waylon was the kind of guy you could count on to do the right thing … once he'd tried everything else. And the man had no sense of humor. He'd turn to me in bed and say, "Marlafaye, I'm about to make you the happiest woman in the world." And I'd look at him and say, "I'm gonna miss you, Waylon." I mean, not even a *smile. (Sighs.)* Life in Tyler, Texas, was no bed of roses … ironic since its claim to fame is being the *Rose Capital of the World*. I landed a job straight out of nursing school and worked for Flip Gawler, perhaps *the* most egotistical doctor in the lower forty-eight and you *know* that competition is stiff. Thirty years I'd work all day for one jackass, then go home and sleep all night with another one. That was my life, carved in stone. It never occurred to me to ask for anything better. But on the very day I found out Waylon had dumped me for Little-Miss-Rinse-And-Spit, I had the good sense to jump up and grab the curveball Fate had thrown me. So I burned those ugly scrubs, set my sights on Savannah, and left the bad memories behind. I became a rep for a liquor distributor, which is not all that different from being a nurse — a visit with me always makes my clients feel better — and I've been here four months. It's *my* town now. *(Beat.)* Sure, it's a little lonely. Nobody promised that startin' a brand new life at fifty-seven would be easy. But I'm workin' on it and thinkin' positive. I get that from my daddy. He always said to bury him in his four-wheel-drive pickup — because "It ain't never been in a hole it couldn't get me out of." Now *that's* positive thinkin'. *(A few bars of country swing play as the pin spotlight goes to black. Marlafaye turns and walks into the light as it comes up on Randa's beautifully appointed second-story verandah of her lovely home. The upstage and stage left exterior walls are butter yellow clapboard with white trim. A door to the kitchen is on the stage left wall. Just downstage of the door is a small cart that serves as a bar. A wicker sofa with brightly colored cushions sits center stage, in front of two interior windows on the upstage wall. Slightly downstage, right and left of the sofa, is a pair of comfortable wicker armchairs. A coffee table is in the center of the seating. A potted palm tree sits at the stage right end of the sofa. An occasional table with a fern on it sits further stage right of the potted palm. A white balustrade extends downstage from the far right upstage wall, with side stairs leading to the street below. Architectural "gingerbread" ornamentation, hanging baskets, and potted greenery complete the Southern elegance of the space. Calls:)* I have arrived — let the party begin! *(Looks around, impressed.)* Man alive, you've got one heck of a house. And your porch! This is what I'm talkin' about!

RANDA. *(Calls from offstage.)* Actually, here it's called a *verandah*.

MARLAFAYE. Yeah? So this is *Randa's verandah*?! *(Laughs. Randa, in a frilly blouse, skirt, heels enters with a bouquet, sets it on coffee table.)*

RANDA. As long as Randa can keep paying the mortgage, it is. What epicurean delight have you brought?

MARLAFAYE. My signature dish — pimento cheese, chock-full

of pickled jalapeños. Just set it out — Velveeta can stand up to a nuclear blast.

RANDA. And yet you never hear that in their ad campaign. Well, this will be … nice with the Gruyère and thyme *cheese* straws I'm making.

MARLAFAYE. Bonus! *(Looks around.)* Yeah, sure is a pretty place, everything's so neat and clean. I'm not like that. Instead of cleaning *my* house, I just turn off the lights. And tell you what, you are brave inviting two strangers over. *(Picks up a small silver candlestick.)* Dottie and I could be a couple of kleptos for all you know. *(Sets it down, walks to stage right railing, looks out.)*

RANDA. Oh, don't be ridiculous. I'm a great judge of character. *(Unseen by Marlafaye, she quickly takes the candlestick to upstage right table, shoves it into the drawer.)*

MARLAFAYE. You see that car out there? It drove past me twice while I was looking for a parking space. Isn't that Dottie? *(Randa joins her.)*

RANDA. Yes, it is. And I keep waving to let her know she's at the correct address, but she doesn't see me. *(Buzzer dings offstage.)* Oops! I've got to check my cheese straws. Would you help get her up here? *(Hurries out.)*

MARLAFAYE. Sure. *(Waves, shouts.)* Dot! *(Louder.)* Dottie! *(Hollers.) Look up! Park that heap and get your butt in here! Time to par-tay!! (Randa races in.)* Hey, I'm pretty sure she heard me.

RANDA. *(Horrified, covers.)* Yes … I'm sure the whole neighborhood did.

MARLAFAYE. So, you found another job yet?

RANDA. No, but I'm sure something will turn up. *(Determined.)* In fact, I thoroughly believe a much better position is out there waiting for me.

MARLAFAYE. That's the spirit! Lucky you're not one of those pathetic crybabies who calls the old boss beggin' for your job back. All that does is convince the folks you used to work for that you're a spineless fool and they were right to have kicked you to the curb.

RANDA. Please. Who would be that desperate? *(Beat.)* So you really think I shouldn't have called?

MARLAFAYE. Shug, I'd say me and my pimento cheese got here just in time. *(Pulls container from purse.)* You know how some people forget to eat? Well, I'm a big advocate of eatin' to forget. Dive in. *(Hands it to her.)*

RANDA. In that case, I hope you brought a lot because I had a dreadful experience this afternoon I just can't shake. At my favorite little market, I ran into the most belligerent woman. She was in the express lane, five-items-or-less, with *eight items!* I kid you not. And when I tactfully called it to her attention, she was vulgar and insulting and loud. It was terrible!

MARLAFAYE. *(Is she for real?)* Wow … where's the National Guard when you need 'em?

RANDA. Exactly! And we wonder how a civilization collapses? *(Dot, in a summer dress, enters side stairs with a large purse, bag, four library books.)*

DOT. *(Staggers slightly.)* Okay, what's spinning — you, me, or the entire room? *(Marlafaye and Randa hurry to help.)*

RANDA. Are you alright?

DOT. I'm fine, dear. I couldn't quite make out the number on your house and had to keep circling the block and it made me a titch dizzy. But, I'm here now and so is the fromage. *(Hands Randa a shopping bag.)*

RANDA. Ah … guess you can never have too much cheese.

MARLAFAYE. *Fromage*, right! I was tryin' to remember what it was you taught all those years.

RANDA. Oh, you taught *French*? I adore all things French. *(Dramatic.) Voulez-vous asseyez pas et se reposer votre grenouille?*

DOT. Actually, I *don't* have a little frog that needs to rest, dear, but *I* certainly could use a sit-down. *(Perches on sofa.)*

RANDA. Guess I am *un peu* … um, rusty. Truth is, I'm a bit out of practice at being a hostess, too.

MARLAFAYE. And I'd offer to help you … *(Hints.)* if I weren't so darned *parched*.

RANDA. Drinks! Of course. I'll be right back. *(Exits with the cheeses. Marlafaye takes the books from Dot.)*

MARLAFAYE. So, they got you drivin' the bookmobile now, Dottie?

DOT. Oh, with Ross gone and so much time on my hands, I've practically lived at the library. I need to return these tomorrow but didn't want someone to break into my car and steal them.

MARLAFAYE. Yep, they keep it pretty quiet about all those folks breakin' into cars to steal large-print library books. *(Checks them.)* Whoa, mama! These are some pretty steamy titles.

DOT. Well, Ross is the one who died, not *me*. *(Randa enters with an opened wine bottle and three glasses on a tray. Sets it on the bar.)*

RANDA. It just so happens, I'd selected a fabulous *French* wine for tonight. *(Hands Dot the bottle. Re: label.)* Does that look familiar?

Perhaps you came across it when you were in France.

DOT. Dear, I taught high-school French in Oklahoma. The only *Paris* I ever got to visit was the one in Texas. *(Tries to read label, holds it as far away as she can. Marlafaye takes it, walks bottle across the room.)*

MARLAFAYE. How about now, Dottie? Any better?

DOT. *(To Randa.)* You don't happen to have that label in large print, do you?

RANDA. It's a Côtes du Rhône Grenache. *(Pours a bit in each glass.)* My brother, Alden, he-who-can-do-no-wrong, recently took a break from walking on water and raising the dead to get married. This was served at the dinner. It's an absolutely unforgettable wine. *(They sip, faces contort. Revulsed, struggle to swallow.)*

DOT. And it still is! *(Marlafaye runs to the balustrade, spits over the side.)*

MARLAFAYE. *(Yells down to the street.)* Oops! Sorry, Sister!

DOT. This strikes me as more of a vinaigrette in search of a salad.

RANDA. I don't know what happened. I let the wine breathe.

MARLAFAYE. Maybe you should've given it *CPR.*

RANDA. This is a disaster! I must've bought a bad year. And it's *all* I have. *(Takes glasses and bottle to lower shelf of bar.)*

MARLAFAYE. *(As she strides to her purse.)* Remain calm, citizens. There's no need to fear … *(Pulls a fifth of bourbon from her purse, strikes superhero pose.)* Whiskey Wonder Woman is here! I give you … Kentucky bourbon at its finest! *(Opens bottle, takes a sniff.)* Ahhh.

DOT. Wow. All I have in *my* purse is keys, lipstick, and Gas-X.

MARLAFAYE. Yeah, but a good liquor rep is *always* prepared.

RANDA. Marlafaye, you are my hero! The nursing profession's loss is our gain. *(Hurries to bar, grabs three clean glasses.)*

DOT. None for me. I never drink hard liquor. Back when we were dating, I overheard Ross say he thought women who drank hard liquor looked cheap.

MARLAFAYE. Well, unless Randa's brother brings Ross back from the other side, I say throw caution to the wind and have yourself a snort.

DOT. Oh … well, maybe just a smidge. *(Randa pours, hands a glass to Marlafaye, pours another, hands it to Dot.)* Mmm … maybe just a smidge more. *(Randa pours again then pours a glass for herself.)*

MARLAFAYE. Girls, here's to livin' single and drinkin' doubles! *(They touch glasses, sip. Dot gasps, coughs.)*

DOT. Fire! I'm on fire! Water, quick! *(Grabs Randa's glass, drinks, goes into another coughing fit.)* Not water … bad idea! *(Gradually gets her breath. Marlafaye pats her on the back.)*

MARLAFAYE. They say you never forget your first time, Dottie.
RANDA. Well, this is turning out to be quite a night. And we definitely have enough cheese for the three of us.
DOT. Oh, that reminds me. There are going to be four of us.
RANDA. *Four* of us?
DOT. Yes! I met this nice woman, the manager of this terrific makeup store, Beautiquity, and she is a fireball! Anyway, she's new in town, too, and she tried that hot yoga class and hated it as much as we did. Well, I told her we were getting together tonight and I think you're really going to like her.
RANDA. *(On the spot.)* Wait. You invited her *here*? *Tonight*?
MARLAFAYE. You *did* say the more the merrier.
RANDA. Well, I only hope … we have enough hors d'oeuvres. I think there'll — *(Sniffs, alarmed.)* My cheese straws! *(Races into kitchen.)*
DOT. Oh, I hope Randa can save them. It's been years since I've had a good cheese straw.
MARLAFAYE. And it's been years since my cholesterol was under three hundred. Considerin' all we've got to eat around here is *cheese*, no chance those numbers will be goin' down tonight. *(Jinx Jenkins, energetic, self-confident, and gregarious, hurries in the side stairs. She wears a low-cut, off-the-shoulder top, short skirt, big jewelry, spike heels, and a purse.)*
JINX. *(Calls.)* Hey, girls! Everyone got your clothes on?
DOT. Jinx! You made it. Jinx Jenkins, this is Marlafaye Mosley.
MARLAFAYE. *Jinx?* That's one humdinger of a name.
JINX. Well, I'm a humdinger of a gal. So, is that Kentucky liquid gold I'm smelling, 'cause, just so you know, bourbon is my favorite color.
MARLAFAYE. I'm thinkin' you're my kind of people. *(Hurries to stage right bar, grabs a glass, pours.)*
DOT. Did you have trouble finding the place?
JINX. Not a bit. I had a late makeover that made me run behind, but it was worth it, my customer told me the cutest joke: An excited woman called her husband at work: "I won the lottery! Come home and pack your clothes!" Husband said, "Ooh! Summer or winter clothes?" Wife says: "All of 'em. I want you out of the house by six!" *(They all laugh.)*
MARLAFAYE. *(Hands Jinx the glass. To Dot.)* Yeah, she's gonna fit in just fine.
JINX. I wasn't sure what to bring, so I went out and got a big slab of Brie. Everyone loves Brie, right? *(Pulls a large chunk of cheese from*

her purse. Dot and Marlafaye exchange a look.)
DOT. How about that? Cheese. I'll get a plate. *(Takes Brie to the bar.)*
MARLAFAYE. And I'll get the Lipitor.
JINX. I ran to the market on my break and all I got was this and seven tangerines. When I got into the five-items-or-less line, the most pretentious, uptight gal I've met in years threw a frothing fit. She went ballistic! *(Marlafaye shoots Dot a worried look.)* I mean, what kind of person is so tightly wound she'd even *care* about that?! *(Laughs. Randa enters, wears two burned oven mitts, carries a cookie sheet, doesn't notice Jinx.)*
RANDA. Okay, it's not a complete disaster, I've saved about thirty percent of the cheese straws. *(Picks one up.)* See, they're just a little too dark, so I guess it will — *(Sees Jinx, stops, gasps. Flares.)* Five-items-or-less!
JINX. *(Bristles. Points.)* Fit thrower! *(They face off.)*
MARLAFAYE. *(Low, to Dot.)* I think the evenin' just got a little more excitin'.
DOT. *(Loosened up by bourbon.)* I'll put twenty bucks on the broad in the cheap jewelry. *(Re: her glass.)* Goodness, this is more potent than I thought.
RANDA. *You're* the "nice woman" Dot told us about?! There must be some mistake!
JINX. The *mistake* was me getting in the five-nut-jobs-or-less line!
MARLAFAYE. *(Steps in.)* Okay, okay. We've all acted the fool in public and regretted it but I refuse to let tonight turn into a waste of good bourbon. Y'all just admit you were both wrong and let's move on.
RANDA. *I* was not wrong! *(Shakes cheese straw in her face.)* This overly-mascaraed rule-breaker is the one who —
JINX. If you don't stop shaking that thing in my face, you're going to draw back a nub. *(Snaps off the cheese straw.)* I didn't come here to — *(Pops it in her mouth, stops cold.)* Oh, my god! This is absolutely divine! You made these yourself?
RANDA. *(Angry.)* Yes, I did! It's the one recipe Grandmother's cook taught me that I can — *(Dawns on her, instantly softens.)* You … You *like* it?
JINX. Yeah, you could make a fortune selling these things.
RANDA. *(Flattered, loving it.)* Really? That's so nice of you to say. If you'd like, I can tell you how to make them.
JINX. Wow. You'd do that for me? That'd be great. And maybe you can explain how to — *(Randa and Jinx get closer as if in conversation, Dot sips her bourbon while lights dim on the verandah. Marlafaye steps*

downstage into a pin spotlight.)
MARLAFAYE. And *that* is the legendary power of Southern cookin' — it can calm nerves, soothe souls — hell, enough butter and love can fix just about anything. This could've been an uncomfortable evening — four strangers gettin' together on a whim, knowing next-to-nothin' about each other — but somethin' just clicked with those half-burnt cheese straws and bourbon and four lonely, middle-aged women who thought nobody wanted to hear what they had to say anymore. We couldn't stop talking — the hours flew by. *(Beat.)* Then somethin' happened I didn't see comin' … *(As she turns, the pin spotlight goes dark and lights come up on the verandah. She joins the others who are repositioned as if time has passed. They laugh raucously.)*
JINX. … Nah, I didn't make it to the gym today. That makes … six years in a row! Woo! *(Throws her arms up in victory. More laughter.)*
RANDA. Well, I for one am very glad we've gotten together tonight. *(To Marlafaye and Dot.)* I mean, at first, when you invited yourselves over, I wasn't sure how it would work out. *(Beat.)* The four of us *are* it. No one else is coming, right?
DOT. *(Laughs.)* No, we're it. And I couldn't agree more. Being alone and new to a place is tough, no palk in the wark … uh, walk in the park.
MARLAFAYE. The gal with the buzz-on makes a good point.
RANDA. I moved here from Augusta years ago and buried myself in work. So in a way, I'm as new to Savannah as you are and I have no clue how to make a life for myself outside my career.
MARLAFAYE. I swear, the older you get, the harder it is to jump-start a new life. How do you find stuff to do? How do you meet someone to go do it with? And how do you do it without running into maniacs, weirdos, and lunatics?
RANDA. Well, obviously —
RANDA/MARLAFAYE/DOT/JINX. *(Indicating the group.)* You can't! *(Everyone laughs, grabs a cheese straw.)*
MARLAFAYE. My point being, you get to a certain age, you are *on your own* and there's nobody around to say, "Here, I can tell you how to do that."
RANDA. Clearly you've never met my grandmother. *(Shivers.)*
JINX. My high school guidance counselor had me convinced a college degree was the answer to everything — success, friends, a good future. Turns out all college did for *me* was wreck my liver *and* my reputation. *(They laugh. Marlafaye gets the bourbon, refills glasses, puts the bottle in her purse.)* But I hung in there and somehow I got myself through Tulane.

MARLAFAYE. Tulane? Are you from the Big Easy?

JINX. I was. But after college, I'd had enough Étouffée to last a lifetime so I split and never went back.

DOT. When we met this afternoon I could've sworn you said you were from Memphis.

JINX. I was for a while. I followed a guy there, followed another guy to Seattle, then I followed Fleetwood Mac to Los Angeles — don't ask — after that I followed a job prospect to Detroit. I followed another guy to Santa Fe, but I left him because he said I never listened to him … at least I think that's what he said.

RANDA. So who did you follow to Savannah?

JINX. A big sister I never knew I had. I found Toni through DNA testing and once we discovered each other, I spent time with her every chance I got. Oh, we had a ball! And talk about a sense of humor. On her sixty-fifth birthday she said, "Jinxy, if my memory gets much worse, I can throw my *own* surprise parties." *(Everyone laughs. Beat.)* But … it did get worse, a lot worse. I moved here to take care of her but sometimes I wonder if she still knows who I am. *(Dot puts her hand on Jinx's shoulder. Jinx rallies.)* Hey, she's the one who taught me it's the happy in life that counts. And that's what I want — more of that. Bring on the happy!

MARLAFAYE. That's *exactly* what I said to my divorce lawyer! *That* and "don't tell me where you dump the body." *(Laughter. Beat.)*

RANDA. Well, I could certainly use some of that *happy*. It was a rare commodity in my family. As my grandmother, Cordelia Covington, the *great nurturer*, is fond of saying, "Life is hard … and we were not put here to have a good time."

JINX. Oh, she sounds like a barrel of laughs. *(To Dot.)* You were right. I can absolutely help everyone in this room.

DOT. I knew it! I'm so glad you came.

RANDA. Excuse me, am I missing out on something?

DOT. When Jinx was helping me with under-eye cream today at Beautiquity, she mentioned she's also a life coach. I almost fell over! Randa, it's exactly what you said could help you.

JINX. That's right. I do beauty makeovers *and* life makeovers.

DOT. And it strikes me that's what we *all* need. *Life* makeovers. I knew this was meant to be, just like the three of us meeting at yoga.

RANDA. *(To Jinx.)* You're here on business?! We've talked about things we probably wouldn't have if we'd known you were here to try to sell us your services. Which, in all honesty, would be more suitable for people

desperate for social interaction, who are lost and unsure of their next moves. *(Thinks about it, exchanges looks with Marlafaye and Dot.)*
MARLAFAYE. *(It strikes a chord.)* In other words … *us.*
DOT. Tell us, Jinx, how many clients have you helped so far?
JINX. Umm … none yet, actually.
RANDA. So, you've never really done this before?
JINX. *Au contraire.* I do it every day. Customers tell me their problems and I dispense advice along with concealer, depilatories, and bleach cream. Makeup artists are just like bartenders, girls. Why do you think it's called a beauty *bar?*
DOT. Well, I do see the correlation.
JINX. So I decided to do some studying and start a side business. I'm ready for a new adventure, too. You're not the *only* middle-aged women looking to change your lives.
MARLAFAYE. Well, how on earth are we gonna do that?
JINX. With a little help from me. Look, between the three of you, you've been widowed, divorced, and fired. You've had the rug pulled out from under you and you've lost your confidence. I've met so many women at the shop who've had similar things happen and they've given up and watched their lives shrivel away. I'm willing to bet none of you wants to settle for some small, quiet life. But to have the wonderful, exciting life you *deserve*, you're going to have to fight for it.
DOT. *(Raises her hand.)* I'd like a wonderful, exciting life, please.
JINX. And tell you what, after six months, if you don't see any change, you don't pay. Is that fair or what?
RANDA. *(Unconvinced, annoyed.)* I'm sorry. This just doesn't seem —
MARLAFAYE. Now, hold on, Randa. I think you might've over-looked the words *"you don't pay."*
DOT. Strikes me as a very sound proposition. I'd welcome a guiding hand.
MARLAFAYE. I'm in. In fact, my therapist always said I could use all the help I can get.
JINX. We can't let life beat us down, girls. The time has come to be fearless. We can still rev up our lives and get back in the game. But at our ages … we've gotta haul ass.
DOT. Come on, Randa. Another point of view couldn't hurt. And no need to be upset, we weren't keeping a secret. Jinx said if this didn't feel like a good fit, she wouldn't even bring it up tonight. *(Wiggles uncomfortably, tugs at her bra strap.)*
JINX. A great place to start is reminding ourselves how to have fun.

And that's *one* thing I do know how to do. *(Idea!)* I know! Maybe the first thing we should tackle is spontaneity. I believe the older we get, the less we're willing to try anything we think will make us uncomfortable. *(Unable to stand it, Dot has worked her red bra off, pulls it out of one sleeve, hurls it on the floor.)*

DOT. Yes, like wearing this darn bra!

JINX. Yeah, mama! Now, see?! *That's* what you need to do.

RANDA. *Take our bras off?*

MARLAFAYE. Okay, but stand back. I wouldn't want any of y'all to get hurt.

JINX. No! I mean be spontaneous. *(Idea!)* Hey, have any of you done the Haunted Savannah Midnight Ghost Tour? It starts just over at Johnson Square. How about let's go do it?

RANDA. What do you mean? *Right now?*

JINX. Well, that *would* be the definition of spontaneity.

MARLAFAYE. Heck, last time I experienced anything spontaneous was on my tenth anniversary. So romantic. Waylon, who spared no expense, turned to me and whispered, "Hey, let's make love with the lights on." And I said, "Waylon, shut the damn car door."

JINX. You in, Dottie? It *is* Savannah, open alcohol containers are legal. We can take our bourbon. *(Crosses to side stairs as Randa snatches up the cheese straws and oven mitts, runs them into kitchen.)*

DOT. *(Laughs.)* Okay! Let's go visit the spirit world. Maybe we'll run into Ross, he can tell me where he hid the key to the boat. *(Joins Jinx, races back, shoves the books into her purse, then grabs her bra.)* Oops! I'd better get back into this. Don't want to scare the ghosts. *(Stuffs bra in her purse.)*

RANDA. *(Reenters from kitchen with her purse.)* So, we're all *really* doing this? You're going to be our life coach?

JINX. Yeah! And we're just getting started! Remember, where there's a will, there's a way.

MARLAFAYE. Not where I come from. In *Texas* you say, where there's a will, *my name* better dang-sure be *in it*! *(Laughter. Randa, Marlafaye, Jinx exit with their bourbon glasses as well as Dot's, as light crossfades to black and downstage right pin spotlight comes up. Dot steps into it.)*

DOT. When I first laid eyes on her, I could see Jinx Jenkins was a gal with a lot on the ball! Okay, I might have overstepped a bit inviting her to Randa's house like I did. But it's been a month now that we've been getting together Friday nights for happy hour and — mostly due to Jinx — I'm beginning to believe Randa and Marlafaye and

I *can* recharge our lives. So far, we've had lots of laughs and great discussions and Jinx has organized some challenging activities … *but* because she's learning as she goes, Jinx *has* hit a bump or two along the way. For example, when she convinced us to do something daring we'd never done before — take a Sunday morning swim in the river — I was all for it. And it really *was* thrilling and oddly peaceful … and then we ran into that swarm of snapping turtles. The screaming didn't really stop until we got to Urgent Care. Poor Marlafaye backed into a very hungry snapper. And where the tattoo on her rear end *used to* read "Love Bug," it now just says "Love ug." *(Brightens.)* But reptile attacks aside, I really do believe things are getting more interesting. And having this feeling in my late sixties is *awesome, Dude! (Beat.)* I think I said that right. Anyway, it's not like I don't still miss my husband, I do. But after I lost Ross, I thought the wonderful retirement life we'd planned was lost *with* him. Well, I still want it! And now, it's starting to feel as if I may finally be getting on with my life. *(Delighted, spunky.)* And that just makes me feel like … like … *dancing! (Pin spotlight goes to black as hot salsa music comes up. Blackout.)*

Scene 3

It's late night. Hot salsa music continues, then fades as lights come up on the verandah. Barefoot, exhausted, Marlafaye and Randa enter through the kitchen door. They wear body-hugging, colorful "salsa" dresses, carry their high-heel dance shoes and purses. Randa leans on the doorframe, massages her neck as Marlafaye limps painfully step-by-step toward the sofa.

MARLAFAYE. Ow. Ow. Ow. Ow. *(Stops, inhales. Continues to sofa.)* Ow. Ow. Ow. Ow. *(Plops down, rubs her feet.)* Not only does salsa burn your guts out when you *eat* it, it durn-near kills you when you *dance* it!
RANDA. *(Limps to armchair, sits.)* I'm sore in places I never even knew I *had* places!
MARLAFAYE. I'm hopin' folks didn't see me crawlin' off the floor after that short fella tried to throw me over his head. *(Beat.)* Tonight

was fun … wasn't it?

RANDA. As opposed to being in a head-on car crash? Absolutely. *(Jinx sashays in kitchen door in a sexy low-cut salsa dress and heels.)*

JINX. Wasn't tonight a blast? *(Does a few dance steps.) Love* that Cuban beat!

MARLAFAYE. You sure were the life of the party. Everyone there adores you. How do you know 'em?

JINX. I never met any of them before. But everybody *loves* a gal with pizzazz.

RANDA. Keeping with the theme of the evening, I got the ingredients for mojitos.

MARLAFAYE. Well don't just talk about it. Drag what's left of you into that kitchen and whip us up some, woman! *(Randa stands, winces.)*

RANDA. *(As she walks to the door.)* Ouch, ouch, ouch, ouch … *(Exits.)*

JINX. *(Sits in armchair, her feet on the coffee table.)* That club was smokin'! Did you catch the action at the bar? I overheard that gorgeous redhead turn down the hunky Latin guy. She said she knew it was old-fashioned, but she's keeping her virginity until she meets the man she loves. He said, "Gee, that must be difficult." She said, "Not for me. But it's got my husband *really* upset." *(They roar with laughter.)*

MARLAFAYE. Honestly, when you first suggested we be brave enough to *do that special thing we'd always wanted to*, I thought that was way up there on the *airy-fairy scale*. But seein' Dot on that dance floor made me think it wasn't such a bad idea after all.

JINX. Yeah. She said what she really wanted to do is go dancing and by gosh, we helped her do it. I'm just sorry she didn't get the chance to kiss a handsome man like she wanted to.

MARLAFAYE. Now wait, when she hyperventilated and blacked out on the dance floor, that EMT guy was kinda cute. And him givin' her mouth-to-mouth *was* kinda like kissin', don't you think?

JINX. Umm … I'll buy it if you will. Hard to believe the only man that woman ever kissed was her husband. Now *that's* a good marriage.

MARLAFAYE. I wouldn't know a thing about that. I knew my marriage was in trouble when I overheard Waylon tellin' his mom, "Some mornings I wake up bitchy. Other mornings I just let her sleep." *(Exhausted, Dot, in a sexy, form-fitting red dress with matching scarf tied around her head, nearly-crippled, enters from the kitchen, has to hold onto furniture to get to the sofa, sits.)*

DOT. What a night. If it wasn't for bunions and gravity, I would've been unstoppable. Anyone want to sign up for their six-week salsa

class? They provide towels, snacks, oxygen — the works.
JINX. So, you'd go back for more?
DOT. *After* I see a chiropractor. And certainly not until I get new prescription lenses. I can't believe I marched right up and asked that tall, odd-looking character for the last dance.
MARLAFAYE. That showed a lot of guts, alright. And all eyes were definitely on y'all when that big ol' homely gal whipped you around the floor like she did.
DOT. Well, Ross always promised we'd take up dancing after he retired, but if that heart attack hadn't gotten him, tonight might have finished him off. *(Randa enters with drinks.)*
RANDA. Alright girls, a little libation from Havana to Savannah. *(The others cheer, take a glass. Randa sits. Dot lifts her glass.)*
DOT. Girls, here's to *you* for doing something *I've* always wanted to do!
MARLAFAYE. And not spending time behind bars for having done it!
JINX. Hear, hear. *(They all touch glasses. Sip.)* Wow, talk about the perfect balance of rum and lime juice. And that mint!
DOT. You know, Randa, if architecture doesn't want you back, you might be able to make it big in bartending.
RANDA. Oh, right. And next time my brother, Alden, is honored for winning some highly-publicized murder case, maybe they'll hire me to mix drinks and bus tables.
JINX. Okay, we helped Dot do her thing, let's keep it going. We are on a roll! What do you think? How about you, Marlafaye? What would you *really* like to do?
MARLAFAYE. Not that it hasn't been interestin' and all, Jinx, but how about we just relax and enjoy our drinks. I mean, don't you think you're pushin' this coachin' idea a *little* hard?
JINX. No. I don't think that at all.
MARLAFAYE. *(Stands, takes hold of her skirt.)* Well, I have a tattoo that begs to differ. Don't make me flash the "Love ug" at you, Jenkins. *(Randa and Dot cover their eyes.)*
RANDA/DOT. Don't make her do it. / We just got over the last viewing!
JINX. Look, I know I'm new at this, but I swear I'm on to something. I went to visit my sister today and … I think she's shutting down. *(Difficult, but forges ahead.)* Now I sit and hold the hand of someone I thought I'd have with me for the next ten, twenty years. But she's not really there anymore. And if that's not a reminder to take advantage of the time we've got and get on with it, I don't know what is.
MARLAFAYE. I get it. But there's no way to do the number one

thing on *my* list. See, when I divorced Waylon, what I hadn't counted on was that when I left, most everyone we knew would take *his* side and *he'd let 'em.* So *he* gets the friends *and* the skank? I don't like being made the villain and I resent it. No ma'am, I will not waste my time or money to go all the way to Texas to vent to a man with delusions of adequacy.

JINX. *(Jumps up.)* Oh, oh! I've got this! I know how to give you the satisfaction of telling Waylon how you feel.

MARLAFAYE. Don't say *phone call.* It wouldn't make me feel a lick better … besides, he's blocked my number anyway.

JINX. That's why you're going to tell him to his face. *(Off their confused looks.)* Role playing!

MARLAFAYE. Oh. I'm not so sure about —

JINX. Come on, let's give it a try. Uh … Randa, you be Waylon.

RANDA. What?! No, I've never done anything like this. I don't know how.

JINX. We agreed we'd do stuff together we've never done before, right?

MARLAFAYE. If she's gonna be Waylon, we gotta make some changes. *(Rummages through her big purse, pulls out a bill cap.)*

RANDA. Forget it. I do not look good in a hat.

DOT. You don't have to worry about that. You're not Randa Covington, you're Waylon Mosley. *(Randa pouts, beat. Takes the cap.)*

RANDA. Okay, fine. *(Puts it on.)* But I feel like an idiot.

MARLAFAYE. See? You're soundin' more like Waylon every minute. *(Grabs a pillow off sofa.)* Here, stuff this under your dress to make a spare tire.

RANDA. *(Snatches the pillow.)* Oh, for heaven's sake. But I won't chew tobacco, don't even think about it. *(Stuffs the pillow under her dress. Marlafaye fluffs up the pillow to make it bigger.)*

JINX. Now we're getting somewhere. *(Positions them facing one another.)* Okay. Say something to Marlafaye, Waylon. *(Silence.)* Randa, *you're* Waylon!

RANDA. Oh! *(Gets into it. Lowers her voice.)* Whut the hell do you wont with me, woman?

DOT. Oh, that's very good. *(Gives her a thumbs up. Encouraged, Randa smiles.)*

RANDA. *(Confident, tougher.)* Spill it, heifer! *(Grins at Dot again.)*

JINX. It's your turn, Marlafaye. This is your chance to face the man who did you wrong and tell him what you want.

MARLAFAYE. *(Deep breath. Then low, menacing.)* I want … to kill you, Waylon. *(Lunges at Randa. Randa recoils, backs across the room.)*
JINX. Go for it, Marlafaye! Go, go! Get it all out!
MARLAFAYE. *(Into it, stalks Randa.)* I worked like a dog tryin' to make our lousy marriage work, never once had a vacation in thirty years. Then you and Twinkerbell sneak off to Six Flags for a big time and charge it all on *my* credit card?! And here I am in my late fifties startin' all over again while you and your child bride carry on with the life I sweated blood to build for *us*?! I'm gonna clean your clock, you dumb butt! *(Lunges for Randa again, chases her through the kitchen door. Randa screams from offstage. Jinx and Dot sit back, enjoy their drinks.)*
JINX. Listen, I'm starting to think I can make a go of this coaching business. Would you three write letters of recommendation for me?
DOT. Of course I'll do that for you. And I can't think of any reason Randa and Marlafaye wouldn't be all for it. *(Randa races into the room screaming, Marlafaye in hot pursuit.)*
RANDA. *(Shouts.)* It's just *role-playing*, Marlafaye! *(Pulls the pillow out of her dress, turns and beats Marlafaye.)* Stop it! Stop! Stop! *(Marlafaye does so. Randa sinks onto the sofa.)*
MARLAFAYE. Hey, that wasn't as stupid as I thought it'd be. *(To Randa and Dot.)* This really works. Y'all should try it. Here, Dot, you want to kill Waylon for a while?
RANDA. No! No more killing Waylon!
MARLAFAYE. Oh. Okay. Sorry. *(Beat.)* I feel *good!* *(Sits, sips her drink.)*
JINX. Hey, more progress. Marlafaye, congratulations on your breakthrough. And Randa, you are so right — you are *not* a hat person. *(Dot and Marlafaye ad lib agreement. Marlafaye puts the hat in her purse.)*
RANDA. Well, tell me something I *don't* know!
DOT. Is everything okay, Randa? You've seemed a little tense tonight.
RANDA. *(Deflated.)* Oh, I'm just tired. Salsa may not be my dance. I haven't perspired this much since I survived Rush Week at Georgia Tech. And — Oh, who am I kidding? Actually, I'm in trouble. *(Deep breath.)* I may lose the house.
JINX. Oh, my gosh! How did this happen?
RANDA. The job search is not going well *at all*. Surprisingly, a forty-nine-year-old female architect who had a very public meltdown is not as highly sought-after as you might think. I used my savings on the down payment and renovation of this place. I never dreamed I'd wind up without an income.
MARLAFAYE. Isn't your old maw-maw loaded? Maybe she could

front you some cash.

DOT. Yes, surely she would. This is an emergency and you're *family*.

RANDA. *My* grandmother, *Cruella de Vil*? Not a chance. However, if Alden asked for a surfboard, she'd gladly buy him a yacht. No, asking her for a loan would only lower her opinion of me, *if* that's possible. In fact, she's coming to town next week to celebrate her ninety-first birthday and I'm just going to stay safely out of sight and avoid the usual demoralizing encounter.

JINX. That's it! I am on fire with ideas here! Am I perfect for this job, or what?! *(To Randa.)* I may know a way you can get back on track with your family. *(Off their looks.)* We're throwing Granny Covington a birthday party that will win her over to your side!

RANDA. Are you out of your ever-lovin' mind?! It's one thing to push us into going swimming and salsa dancing, now you want me to bake a cake for *Satan*?!

JINX. Remember how I said now's the time to be fearless? Well, you've got to gamble big to win big. This one little gesture could change your whole life

MARLAFAYE. She's right, Randa! 'Cause, girl, your life's so pitiful right now, the only way you can go is up!

DOT. Marlafaye, dear, no one really likes to be reminded her life is in the crapper. *(Randa slumps in exasperation.)*

JINX. *(Puts one arm around each, Marlafaye and Dot.)* Okay, *this* would be a good example of why *I* get to be the life coach and you two *don't. (Lights crossfade as Randa, Dot, and Marlafaye quickly exit into the kitchen with shoes, purses, mojito glasses, as downstage left pin spotlight comes up. Jinx walks into the light.)* Randa continued to be a little doubtful about my idea of the birthday party. But eventually, she got on board and we threw ourselves into it, spent the week getting ready for the *big do* in Randa's elegant dining room — we laid in caviar, the finest oysters, salmon mousse, all of her old granny's faves. Oh, and champagne, of course — doesn't hurt knowing a certain Texan who gets a steep discount. And I've got a great feeling about this. We'll have a ball and maybe, just maybe, Randa can *finally* win the old girl over. Look, I'm not kidding myself, it's a serious responsibility when someone puts her trust in you, but I was born for this! And it's a fantastic feeling that I might actually be able to help change people's lives for the better … which is topped only by the thrill of getting good liquor on the cheap! Woo-hoo! *(Left pin spotlight fades, then Jinx exits into kitchen.)*

Scene 4

A week later, late afternoon. Lively harpsichord music plays as a pin spotlight comes up downstage right on Randa, now in an attractive top over her salsa dress.

RANDA. So, the big day finally came. And with the girls behind me, I was confident, I was focused. I was a rock … *(Her bravado fades, jittery.)* That is, until I heard that evil voice screeching from downstairs. The same voice that has turned my blood to ice for as long as I can remember. *(Mimics her grandmother's demanding tone.)* "Miranda! I'm here. I don't have all day. Where are you?" *(Back to her own voice.)* I wavered slightly, but pulled it together like a champ. *(Calls, sweetly.)* "Up here, Grandmother, on the verandah." And I knew there was no going back — I *had* to make this work. And then … *she appeared. (As the lights come up on the verandah, an elegantly dressed elderly woman in a hat, with a stylish walking stick, enters, her face not visible to the audience.)* I swallowed hard, then said to her, "Grandmother, I'm glad you're here. And I know it's your birthday and I just wanted to say … " *(Jinx, Dot, Marlafaye, all in tops over their salsa dresses, burst out of the kitchen and shout.)*
RANDA, JINX, DOT, and MARLAFAYE. Surprise!! *(Grandmother gasps, clutches her chest, crumples to the floor. Beat. They freeze, stare at Grandmother in disbelief. Marlafaye hurries over, takes her pulse.)*
MARLAFAYE. Huh. *Dead's* not really the reaction we were hopin' for. *(Randa, Jinx, and Dot all go to the body, stare down at it a moment.)*
RANDA. Oh, god. We killed Grandmother.
DOT. But on the bright side, we *did* surprise her. *(The women clutch each other.)*
JINX. Girls, when you write my letters of recommendation, let's just leave this little part out, okay? *(Blackout.)*

End of Act One

ACT TWO

Scene 1

Weeks later, late afternoon. Up-tempo jazz plays as downstage right pin spotlight comes up. Randa, wearing a dressy black skirt and top, steps into the light. She carries a small box.

RANDA. It's been said, "The more you complain, the longer God makes you live." Grandmother died *on her ninety-first birthday* — obviously even *He* couldn't take it anymore. Come to find out she had every cardiac issue imaginable, but, being Grandmother, she didn't bother telling anyone in the family about it. Frankly, it was a surprise to me to find out she *had* a heart. But die she did and thus began the endless tributes over the past six weeks that elevated her, in death, to sainthood. Being the dutiful doormat granddaughter, I showed up for all of it — the wake, the funeral, the memorial, the renaming of the park, and, today, the final indignity, the reading of the will. And because no Covington Family gathering is complete without "helpful" comments on my unrelenting single status, my eccentric Aunt Juliette cornered me with more words of wisdom. She said, "Miranda, darling, you must keep this in mind — it's important to have a man in your life who can repair things; it's important to have a man in your life who can make you laugh; it's important to have a man in your life who's good in bed. *(Lower.)* And it's very important that these three men never meet, or you could end up dead." *(Sighs.)* My family tree has incredibly twisted roots. *(A few bars of up-tempo jazz play as pin spotlight goes to black. Randa pockets the box, turns, and walks into the light as it comes up on the verandah.)*
JINX. *(Offstage.)* Yoo-hoo! Anybody home?
RANDA. *(Goes to side stairs, calls down.)* Yes, I just walked in! Come on up! I'm desperate to spend time in the company of sane people — *(Jinx glides in from side stairs dressed in a scarlet Renaissance costume: low, low square neckline, tops of the sleeves are overly puffed and just below the puff become straight and tight to wrist, a lace-up black corset is over the bodice*

and floor-length skirt. This is topped off with a tall, cone-shaped scarlet headpiece, a veil attached at the tip.) And it appears I'm out of luck.

JINX. It feels like you've been gone forever. You'll never believe what we got into.

RANDA. Uh, the Witness Protection Program?

JINX. No, a Renaissance Faire. They were having one at Hilton Head and I've been way too embarrassed to admit I've always wanted to go to one.

RANDA. But why would you be embarrassed? *(Dot enters in a similar over-the-top Renaissance sapphire-blue princess costume, carries a small jug. Her headpiece is topped with not one but two tall cones tipped with veils.)* I withdraw the question.

DOT. Good morrow, fair Miranda of the Verandah. *(Holds out the jug.)* Prithee take this vessel of libation for thine bar and we shall quaff it anon.

JINX. *(To Dot.)* Showoff. *(Randa takes the jug.)*

RANDA. How much fun that you all got to dress up and look so beautiful!

DOT. Well … *(Jinx and Dot exchange a look.)* *Some* of us got to. *(Marlafaye, not at all happy, enters side stairs in a jester's costume: fool's cap with three points, jingle bells at the end of each, overshirt made of two different-colored/patterned fabrics, pieced together in sections, matching trousers, one leg one fabric, the other the different fabric. She carries a mock scepter with jingle bells attached.)*

MARLAFAYE. Trust me, I'm not nearly as happy as I look.

JINX. We keep telling you, that outfit's adorable.

MARLAFAYE. Don't make me whomp you upside the head with this stick. I wanted some pretty today and *was* about to rent the last dress when Jinx said my shoe was untied. While I fixed it, another gal stepped up, took it out from under my nose. *This* was all they had left. *(Sits on sofa, pouts.)*

DOT. Prithee, be of good cheer, merry jester.

MARLAFAYE. I'm warnin' you … *(Shakes scepter.)* there's plenty of this stick to go around.

RANDA. *(Re: jug.)* What *is* this?

JINX. Mead. You know, fermented honey and water. They were selling it at the faire. I thought, we have got to try *this*.

RANDA. Alright, then. I'll check to see if I have any … flagons. *(Crosses to bar, gets glasses, pours.)* So, you all had a great time?

JINX. Well … I don't know that we'd ever need to go to another one.

(Sits on sofa with Marlafaye.)

DOT. It *was* quite an experience. People were gnawing at huge turkey legs hot off a spit so I gave one a try and blistered the devil out of my tongue. I had to walk around with a mouth full of ice the rest of the afternoon. *(Sits in armchair.)*

MARLAFAYE. Well, that *was* bad, but I think my incident gets the sympathy vote. I was chased up a tree by a wild animal.

JINX. It was a chicken! You're from Texas. You cannot be afraid of poultry.

MARLAFAYE. Hey, just 'cause I talk like a hick doesn't mean I was raised on a farm. Those things have claws!

JINX. *(To Randa.)* Anyway, we really missed you, kid. So … *(Delicately.)* How did it go?

RANDA. *(Gives them drinks.)* Well, unless they decide to add Grandmother's head to Mount Rushmore, it's finally over and I'm still standing.

MARLAFAYE. Bully for you for survivin' your family and gettin' through it. *(Holds up her glass.)* Here's mead in your eye! *(They toast, sip. Beat.)*

RANDA. Wow. This really isn't so horrible.

MARLAFAYE. The very words I said on my weddin' night. *(Off their looks.)* Ah, come on. Sex is like a brownie — when it's good, it's really good. And when it's bad … it's still pretty good!

DOT. This is tasty … of course, that turkey leg was so salty, I'd drink dishwater right now.

RANDA. Oh, there's one other thing — at the reading of the will, I got a door prize. *(Pulls the box from her pocket.)* Of course, Alden used the solemn occasion to announce he's running for State Senate, which will be much easier now that he's inherited Grandmother's *entire* estate. *(Holds up the box.)* Except for my little box.

DOT. Your grandmother left you a box? Is anything in it?

RANDA. Probably a poisoned dart. I just haven't had the nerve to open it and confirm my suspicion.

DOT. But maybe she wanted to make up for the two of you having such a bad relationship all those years. It could be something *good.*

RANDA. I seriously doubt it. This is the woman I turned to when I was thirteen and asked, "Grandmother, as I get older, do you think I'll lose my looks?" Her response was, "Yes, if you're lucky."

JINX. Which leads me to believe you don't bear a grudge against me for the fatal birthday surprise?

RANDA. Grudge? I only wish you'd come up with that idea twenty years ago. *(The others howl, lift their glasses to her.)*
MARLAFAYE. I'm thinkin' Coach here would say it's time to hitch up your big-girl britches and open the dang box.
JINX. That's exactly what I'd say, if I spoke Texan.
RANDA. O-kay. *(Deep breath. Starts to take the lid off, stops.)* I can't do it. Here. *(Hands it to Jinx, who opens box, pulls out a note.)*
JINX. *(Reads.)* "I bequeath this to my only granddaughter, Miranda, although it's doubtful she'll ever own a decent dress with which to wear it."
RANDA. Yep, it's from her, alright. *(Wads up the note, stuffs it in her pocket. Jinx pulls a brooch from the box. They gasp, stare at it.)*
DOT. Zounds and forsooth! Thou art the recipient of *bling*!
RANDA. It's probably paste or glass. Trust me, Alden got all the heirlooms.
JINX. Wait a minute. The guy I followed to Seattle was a gemologist … *and* into naked frisbee golf, but *that* story would take a whole lot more than mead. *(Studies it.)* Hey, do you have a magnifying glass?
RANDA. Somewhere in my office. *(To Marlafaye.)* Come help me look. Let's just get this over with.
MARLAFAYE. Hey, that's the *other* thing I said on my weddin' night. *(She grabs the jug as she and Randa exit into the kitchen.)*
JINX. Oh, before I forget, can you drive these costumes back over to the rental place tomorrow?
DOT. Oh. Uh … actually, no. *(Off Jinx's look.)* I … lost my driver's license. I failed the vision test — for the fourth time. We were having so much fun today, I didn't want to bring it up.
JINX. *(Arm around her.)* Listen, one of my customers, who couldn't paint on a decent set of eyebrows to save her neck, is an ophthalmologist. I'll call her first thing tomorrow and get you in. We're going to take care of this, okay? *(Dot nods in agreement as Randa and Marlafaye enter from kitchen.)*
RANDA. *(Hands Jinx a magnifying glass.)* I still think this is a waste of effort. The old snake wouldn't have left me anything of value.
JINX. *(Inspects brooch, gasps.)* Then she screwed up, because these boulders are real diamonds and the brooch is *signed*. Get this sucker to a jeweler a.s.a.p., sell it and save your home!
RANDA. *(Takes it, her hand trembles.)* Are you saying the only way anyone in my family has ever come to my aid was unknowingly, unwillingly, and totally by accident? *(Thrilled!)* I'll take it! *(They all*

hug, celebrate.)
MARLAFAYE. Woo-hoo!!! I'll bet the old girl's twirlin' in her grave like a giant turkey leg on a spit!
DOT. Me thinketh this momentous occasion deserveth more than mere mead! What sayeth we go downtown and hit-eth the bars?
JINX. Yeah! Why not? We're Renaissance women. We can do anything we want … *(They head for kitchen door.)* As long as we drink responsibly.
MARLAFAYE. Absolutely! And any joker knows "drink responsibly" means *don't spill it*! *(Laughter. Lively Renaissance music comes up as Jinx, Dot, and Randa take magnifying glass, box, and brooch, exit into kitchen, and light fades to black as downstage right pin spotlight comes up. Marlafaye crosses downstage, walks into spotlight, removes the fool's cap.)* I guess this is the way it happens — *life*, that is. One day you're locked in a sweatbox with some health nuts thinkin' you're either gonna blow your groceries or stroke out. Next thing you know, you've got yourself a handful of potential friends. Funny how that works. It's been a few months since we started gettin' together and I gotta say, all four of us *seem* to be "re-energizin'" our lives — which is a loosey-goosey way of sayin' "*gettin' off our cans* and takin' care of business." 'Course Jinx forcin' the four of us to traipse off to the opera one night was nothin' but a bust. I mean, who sings for twenty minutes when they're dyin'?! And it wasn't even in English! Other than that, it's all been pretty good. But right now, there's trouble a-brewin'. Jinx has given us a "courage challenge" that's way over the top. She said we all had to do somethin' good for our hearts, but I told her no way, no how was I eatin' *kale*! That stuff is some kind of nasty. Then she explained she *meant* we all had to suck it up and get ourselves dates for *Valentine's Day* — which is almost as bad as eatin' kale. *(Sighs.)* But I did it. We all did. *(Beat. Guiltily.)* I kinda run hot and cold about *my* date and even though I've been thinkin' about him for a while now, it makes me nervous. I know what I'd *like* it to lead to, and I also know that's puttin' the cart before the horse. *(Confident.)* So I'm not tellin' the girls much about this 'cause I'm not about to tempt Fate. *(Puts fool's cap on at a jaunty angle.)* No sirree Bob… my mama didn't raise no *fool*! *(Looks down at her costume, realizes what she's wearing, sighs. Blackout.)*

Scene 2

Valentine's Day, late afternoon. An up-tempo love song plays as lights come up on the verandah. Jinx enters from the kitchen in a form-fitting pair of black evening trousers, a fancy, low-cut evening top, sparkly jewelry, heels, carries an evening purse, a bottle of nail polish, crosses to an armchair, sits.

JINX. *(Calls.)* Come on, Dot, let me paint your fingernails! Since this is your first date in forty years, you're going to look like the wanton woman you were born to be. *(Dot, who wears dangly earrings, capri pants, cute top and heels, enters from kitchen with two glasses of tea.)*
DOT. I love this makeover you gave me … what I can see of it. Randa made us some tea. It's a big night, let's start it on a caffeine high. *(Hands her a glass.)*
JINX. Give me those paws, Haigler. *(Holds up nail polish.)* I'm lacquering you up with Passion's Promise.
DOT. *(Happy, sits.)* Ooh. Happy Valentine's Day to me! I intend to knock Captain Rusty right off his pins. *(Jinx paints Dot's nails.)*
JINX. Now, how long have you been flirting with the Captain and why didn't you bother to tell us?
DOT. It's not *flirting*. I call it *chatting with intent*. You know I walk down to the marina every morning. Well, I always see him working on his boat — *Pretty Eileen* — and one time I had the nerve to say hello. We've been *chatting* ever since. *(Confidential.)* And yesterday he gave me … a grouper.
JINX. *(Teases.)* Well, aren't *you* the fast woman in a slow town. So you hooked him and now you're reeling him in.
DOT. Oh, I'm not *that* fast. Let's just get through dinner tonight. He's taking me to the Crab Shack and the good news is, if he's a slob and dribbles food on his shirt, I'll never see it.
JINX. *(Lowers her voice.)* So those drops aren't helping your vision at all?
DOT. Not really. Maybe this new specialist will have an answer. But I'm not worrying about that now because this evening's going to be beautiful.

JINX. Atta girl. Here, give me that other hand. No one leaves this house without looking totally sexy and sophisticated. *(Randa hurries in from kitchen in slacks, a gaudy, low-cut sequin top, a matching sequin scarf tied in her hair.)*
RANDA. *(Strikes a pose.)* Okay, Jinx, how do I look?
JINX. Like a disco ball with feet. Take it off. Then burn it.
RANDA. What? You said to go for something daring and exotic.
DOT. Dear, I think she meant more stylish and haughty than slutty and naughty.
JINX. Now, rip that ugly thing off and try again. It's getting late!
RANDA. I feel disaster looming. *What* do I have in common with the guy who roasts the coffee beans I overpay for? Why did I agree to this?
DOT. Your date won't be worse than one I had with the pitcher of our college baseball team. His Impala broke down on our date and since he was worried about his precious pitching arm, *I* got to push the car five miles back to campus. That just ruined baseball *and* Chevrolets for me forever! *(Laughter.)*
JINX. Well, I hope my first date with an athlete turns out better. I have high hopes because my date tonight's with a biker.
DOT. Ooh, Harley?
JINX. No. Schwinn. He owns the bike shop two doors down from Beautiquity. And I'm telling you, the man can wear some Spandex. He knows how to stretch it 'til it fairly screams for mercy! *(They laugh. Jinx turns to Randa.)* Wait. What are you still standing here for? Get in there and de-glitter yourself. Now, now, now! *(Randa hurries into kitchen.)*
DOT. How can that talented woman still be unemployed?
JINX. Beats me. Even with the cash from that brooch, she could still use a boost. I hope her date at least brings her flowers. *(Finishes Dot's nails.)*
DOT. Oh, speaking of which, did your sister like your bouquet?
JINX. I think so. I read her the Valentine but it didn't seem to register. She must figure I'm just this pleasant stranger who drops by with tangerines.
DOT. *(Pats her hand, upbeat.)* Well, that may be the role you get to play in this part of her life. And I think you do it very well. *(Fans herself.)* Can you explain why it's so hot in Savannah in February? This heat isn't helping Marlafaye's nerves. She seems pretty wound up about this evening.
JINX. We're all anxious, but really it's just an exercise — one dinner

on one evening with one guy. We can get through this. *(Pops nail polish in purse.)*

DOT. *(Low.)* This may sound odd, but do you think it's possible that she couldn't get up the nerve to ask someone out? Maybe she's faking it and just going through the motions to keep from disappointing us.

JINX. Well, I don't think she's acting abnormal or anything. *(Marlafaye races in, wears a skirt, full slip, and heels, carries a blouse and a spray can. She paces manically back and forth as she rants.)*

MARLAFAYE. What genius decided to make this shirt out of acrylic polyester plastic crap?! I put this thing on and look like a shrink-wrapped Vienna sausage. It sticks to my skin and shows every bulge I've got. *(Re: the can.)* And *this* is worthless. I could be soakin' this rag in weed killer for all the good this anti-static spray has done! *(Sprays the blouse, then supports her bust with one arm, whirls the blouse over her head to dry it.)*

JINX. *(Low, to Dot.)* Okay. Maybe she's acting just a *tad* abnormal.

DOT. That's going to be beautiful on you, Marlafaye. Just put it on, maybe get a belt and cinch it up real tight for a different style.

MARLAFAYE. *(Whirls the blouse faster.)* Do I *look* stupid?

JINX/DOT. Yes! *(Randa enters through kitchen door in slacks, fuzzy bedroom slippers, and a great-looking, elegant dressy top.)*

JINX. *(Spots Randa.)* Wow, where have you been hiding *that*?

RANDA. Alden's campaign manager sent it to me with instructions to wear it at the "loving family" photo session next week. I say, if it's good enough for the future senator, it's good enough for the coffee roaster … who will probably think I'm not good enough for him … which is why I've *just* decided I'm not going. *(Starts for kitchen door. Jinx grabs her.)*

JINX. Okay, that does it. Will you two stop freaking out?! Marlafaye, that blouse is fine and stop spraying that mess or all of our *insides* will be static free! *(Takes Randa by the shoulders.)* And you listen to me, Randa Covington. You're an intelligent, beautiful, and interesting person in your own weird way. Your date sounds like a nice guy, you're going to your favorite fancy restaurant, you'll have a great time. You can do this. Now, tell yourself you deserve it. Say it!

RANDA. Well, I … I guess I *do* deserve it. *(Enthusiasm explodes.)* You're right! I can do this, Coach! *(Jinx, Dot pat her on the back, encourage her.)* This will be good! I'm on it! *(Slaps high-fives with the others, a prizefighter, ready for the ring.)* Yeah! I'm smokin' — Not *literally*, but … you know —

JINX. Yeah, we know! Now go put on some real shoes. Your higher-end restaurants tend to frown on fuzzy slippers. *(Randa looks down, groans.)*

RANDA. I knew I'd overlooked something. *(Checks for her bra.)* Good, just the shoes. And I'm so late! I'll get my things and go out the front. Lock up when you leave. We'll meet back here for the debriefing. *(Races out kitchen door.)*

JINX. *(To Marlafaye.)* Okay, Tex. One breakdown averted. Now it's time for *you* to sling the meat on the table. What's up?

MARLAFAYE. You mean besides my blood pressure? Nothin'. Why?

DOT. Dear, is it possible you've just concocted a *mystery* man and once we walk out of here, you're going straight home to put your feet up?

MARLAFAYE. What?! No! I … You don't … *(Gives up.)* Look, there are just some things a woman wants to keep to herself.

JINX. However, *you* are not that woman. I know more intimate details of your life than I do mine. I can tell you how old you were when you got your first French kiss … and where you threw up afterwards.

MARLAFAYE. *(Nervous.)* Okay, okay. Maybe I just thought y'all would tell me it's a bad idea and that I shouldn't do it.

DOT. We would *never* discourage you. We're here to support you.

MARLAFAYE. Okay … my mystery man is … Waylon.

JINX/DOT. *What?!*

JINX. It's a bad idea!

DOT. Don't do it!

MARLAFAYE. See, this is exactly why I didn't tell you!

DOT. How on earth did this happen?!

MARLAFAYE. Look, I was gonna invite a guy on a date, just like you said, but, out of the blue, Waylon called. I haven't heard from him in forever! And he said he was coming to town because he's *got* to see me and has somethin' *really important* to say. Think about it — Waylon needs to tell me somethin' *on Valentine's night* and he's drivin' halfway across the country to do it. Y'all, the man's gonna finally give me the apology I deserve and have been wantin' to hear! I wouldn't miss this for the world!

JINX. You can't trust him, he cheated on you.

DOT. She's right. You'll only get hurt again. You need to listen to your life coach on this.

MARLAFAYE. Well, the life coach is *wrong*. I'm goin'. *(Brandishes spray can at them as if it's a gun.)*

JINX. *(Snatches the blouse.)* Well, you can't go half-naked! *(Marlafaye lunges for the blouse. Jinx wads it up, runs it to Dot, calls.)* I'll block the kitchen door! *(Passes blouse to Dot, who grabs it, runs the other way. Marlafaye chases Dot.)* Here Dot! Here! *(Dot throws the blouse into the air. Marlafaye jumps up, snatches it.)*

MARLAFAYE. Ha, ha! Can't stop me now! *(Exits down side stairs. Dot starts to follow.)*

DOT. Hurry, Jinx! We've got to catch her!

JINX. Wait Dot, let her go! She's a hard-headed Texan and she's going to do what she's going to do.

DOT. *(Sighs.)* You're right, dear. I suppose there *are* worse things than spending Valentine's Day with your lying, cheating ex-husband who took all your money and ran off with a twenty-three-year-old. *(They look at each other a beat, then:)*

DOT/JINX. Naaaah!! *(Dot exits side stairs. Light crossfades to black as a slow, sexy love song plays. The downstage right pin spotlight comes up. Jinx takes a couple of dance steps into it.)*

JINX. I can truthfully say I'm a sucker for a lot of things — baby panda videos, drinks with tropical fruit and umbrellas in them, bobble-head dolls of former First Ladies … and Valentine's Day. I take one look at the cut-out hearts and tubby little cupids and ads with lovers kissing on the beach, and in spite of myself, I fall for it hook, line, and sinker every single year. Maybe it's one of those hope-springs-eternal things. And yet, never *once* have I ever had a decent date on Valentine's Day. And as low as that bar is set, I think I achieved a new record with this one tonight. Turns out, Mr. God's-Gift-To-Spandex is a world-class narcissist! We'd just been seated at a great table, and I said, "What a gorgeous view, right?" He agreed with such gusto I whipped my head around and saw he was admiring his own reflection in the back of a spoon! And all the guy could talk about were *bicycles*. He spent the entire meal quoting stats on competition bicycle construction right down to the carbon-fiber disc wheels. By the time he extolled the virtues of shaving his legs to achieve more aerodynamic flow, I wanted to beat him to death with a tire pump. But now I realize the lesson I was supposed to learn from this — *never* date a guy whose calves are better-looking than *yours!* *(The pin spotlight fades to black as lights come up on the verandah, later that night. Dot is at the bar as Jinx walks into the light.)*

DOT. I'm pouring you some of this nice Madeira I brought.

JINX. Obviously I could use it. *(Checks her watch.)* Randa's not back yet?

DOT. Let's hope it means she's having a fabulous time. I'm so sorry you didn't.

JINX. Yeah. So am I. *(Pulls her compact out of her purse, checks out her mascara.)* It just knocks me out. How could anybody be that vain? *(Touches up her lipstick, puts compact away.)*

DOT. *(Covers a smile.)* You got me. *(Hands her a tiny cordial glass. Randa bursts in from the kitchen on an adrenaline rush.)*

RANDA. Oh, my God! This has to be the most wonderful night of my life!

JINX. What happened? Are you in love, getting married, what?

RANDA. It was magnificent! I'm still trying to process it. Well, I was poring over the menu and someone tapped me on my shoulder. I looked up and it was Douglas, my former boss.

DOT. *(Gasps.)* Oh, no! I hope you didn't make a scene.

RANDA. I would never do that at Arcadia. The maître d' was always so generous to me when I entertained clients there. He never failed to send over this delicious herbed butter every time I —

JINX. Get back on track, Covington.

RANDA. Sorry. At first he said nothing, but Douglas had this *look* on his face. So I quickly — but firmly — reminded him the restraining order only applies to the office building and doesn't bar me from other public places.

JINX. Gee, makes you wonder how many times *that* romantic phrase was uttered on this special night.

RANDA. Anyway, he said he was just about to call me. Turns out, one of Douglas' biggest clients — for whom I designed two excellent commercial buildings in addition to his summer home, by the way — hired Douglas for his newest project contingent on *my* taking the lead. Douglas panicked and told him I was out for some personal time — which I suppose theoretically is true. But the client said if Doug can't deliver me, the deal's off.

DOT. I hope you told him you wouldn't do the job for any price. Serves him right.

RANDA. Are you kidding? I haven't even had a nibble from the job market in months. I said I absolutely *would* head up the project! But since I knew I had old Douggie over a barrel, I also told him I would do it only as an independent consultant *and* … for double the money! *(They cheer as Randa does a victory dance.)*

JINX. That is fantastic! *(Stops her.)* But this time around you've got to remember that there's more to life than work.

RANDA. Oh, I know that — there's also *revenge!* (*Resumes the dance.*)
DOT. (*To Jinx.*) Well … can't argue with that.
RANDA. I didn't budge, I held my own. When we'd finished working out the details of the deal nearly two hours later, I made darn sure Douglas ordered the most expensive cognac they had to celebrate.
DOT. All of this must've been very impressive to your date.
RANDA. (*Stunned silence. Then, explodes.*) Oh, my god! *My date!* (*Jumps to her feet.*) I left the coffee roaster alone at our table! (*Races into kitchen.*)
JINX. And we were *this close* to a happy ending for everyone in that story.
DOT. Well … *C'est le vie et encore il est bon.*
JINX. You said a mouthful, sister. (*Sighs.*) Looks like her date didn't go any better than mine. Oh, well, maybe in the next place I move to, I'll finally find Mr. Almost-Good-Enough. (*Dot stares at her a beat.*)
DOT. I wanted to ask you about that. Why *do* you move around so much?
JINX. (*Baffled.*) *Why?* I just have. When I grew up I just kept moving. Who knows? Maybe I'm just looking for *that wonderful thing.*
DOT. (*Delicately.*) But will you know it when you find it? (*Stumped, Jinx stares at her a beat. Deflated, Randa enters from kitchen.*)
RANDA. He'd already left a message and never wants to see me again. If I ever *do* show my face my coffee beans will cost an extra six dollars a pound.
JINX. (*Tries for a silver lining.*) Ah, but *now* you can afford it!
RANDA. That's right. (*Brightens.*) Score! (*High-fives all around.*)
DOT. (*Takes ice tea glasses to the bar.*) Well, *my* night wasn't quite as thrilling as yours, Randa. But Captain Rusty is a lovely man. We laughed — I loved his stories — dinner was scrumptious, but later the evening took … an odd turn.
RANDA. *How* odd? Dragging you to a karaoke bar *odd* or showing you pictures of his cats dressed in *Star Trek* costumes *odd?*
DOT. Actually, Captain Rusty … took me to a cemetery.
JINX. No "My place or yours?" just "Let's hit the bone yard, baby." I don't know, Dot, that's kinda kinky.
DOT. At first I was a bit uneasy, but I *did* find out who *Pretty Eileen* was — his late wife. They were very happily married, like Ross and I were. So in a peculiar but touching kind of way, it was almost as if he wanted me to "meet" her. (*Jinx and Randa share a look.*) It was very … sweet.

RANDA. So, are you going to see him again?

DOT. I thought I might until he took me in his arms in the moonlight and said those magic words — "I'll bet you were really good-looking when you were young." And now he's just as dead to me as pretty Eileen.

JINX. How come crazy people know exactly how to find us? *(Just then, Marlafaye bursts in the side stairs, storms over to the bar. Jinx indicates Marlafaye.)* You see what I mean?

MARLAFAYE. I know y'all are probably still ticked at me, but I need a drink and someone to talk to — in that order. Who's up for it?

JINX. *(Frosty.)* Yeah? Well, what if none of us are?

MARLAFAYE. Y'all want to know what happened with me and Waylon or not?

JINX. *(Instant flip, pats sofa.)* Girl, sit right here and don't spare the details.

RANDA. Oh, my God, your date was with your *ex*?! *(Hurries to bar.)* Save some of that for me. *(Marlafaye fills two tiny cordial glasses, Randa knocks back hers.)* Okay. Go for it. *(Randa quickly plops down on the sofa.)*

MARLAFAYE. *(Sips.)* When I got there Waylon was already seated which I thought was a good sign, but then I saw he was already workin' his way through three fried eggs and a plateful of scattered, smothered, and covered. The man always eats like a hog when he's nervous so I knew whatever he had on his mind was —

JINX. Wait! I'm still wrapping my head around the fact he'd *already* ordered and was *eating*, but are you telling us he invited you out for Valentine's Day at a *Waffle House*?

MARLAFAYE. Hey, that's high-end gourmet for Waylon. If food wasn't shoved at him through a car window, he'd die of starvation.

RANDA. Obviously, I'm a little late to this party, but why on earth did you agree to see him?

MARLAFAYE. Look, I know it's nuts, but layin' in my bed all these nights since I moved here made me feel lonely and vulnerable. We all know how hard it is to start a new life from scratch, it feels kinda like a free fall, nothin's *familiar*. And for a few seconds over the last couple months, I'm ashamed to admit that I was almost … well … missin' him. *(The others shudder in unison.)* I said *almost*! Trust me, the feelin' was gone the minute I saw him talk with his mouth full of cheese grits.

DOT. You know, none of us is getting any younger. Maybe you could

fast-forward this story. Did you hear the words you wanted to hear?
MARLAFAYE. Actually the words I *heard* were "I need to borrow ten thousand dollars." *(The others gasp.)*
JINX. *That's* why he drove all this way to see you?!
MARLAFAYE. Wait! There's more. *(The others lean forward in anticipation.)* The next thing he said was something I couldn't have anticipated in a million years and it absolutely knocked the wind outta me. *(Deep breath.)* Turns out he and the hygienist are … *(Softer, without emotion.)* gonna have a baby. *(Turns upstage, covers her face, her shoulders begin to shake. The others share concerned looks. Dot goes to her, strokes her back.)*
DOT. *(Gently.)* It's going to be alright. *(Marlafaye slowly turns around. She hasn't been crying at all, just trying to control hysterical laughter.)*
MARLAFAYE. *(Guffaws.)* You bet your bodacious butt it is!
RANDA. And you're really okay with all this?
MARLAFAYE. *Okay?!* I couldn't be happier! I've wanted that man to get his comeuppance and, oh, brother, is he ever gonna get it now! Midnight feedin's, potty training — not much *us time* for the newly-weds. And do the math, ladies. When Baby hits kindergarten, ol' Pappy will be sixty-five on Medicare, pushin' eighty when Junior steals his first car, and a proud ninety when the kid finally gets his GED. Oh, there's so much for Waylon to look forward to in his golden years. Yeah. He *deserves* this happiness! *(The others laugh.)*
JINX. Well, you didn't get your apology, but it looks like you got something a whole lot better. Consider that toilet flushed.
MARLAFAYE. You know, maybe it was my destiny to go to that Waffle House tonight. I finally realize you can't let your past block your plans for the future. And I — for one — think the future looks pretty dang bright. *(Jinx pounds Marlafaye on the back.)*
JINX. I am so proud of you. And I am *so* stealing what you just said to use on any new clients I get!
RANDA. What a night. We all had dates — weird ones, but we did it! *(Checks her watch.)* And I'm pleased to announce, it's seven after midnight and it's no longer Valentine's Day! *(They cheer, quickly gather their things.)*
MARLAFAYE. After midnight? Hey, I gotta get up early tomorrow and sell some hooch. Can I give you a lift home, Dottie?
DOT. Oh, sure. I've got tai chi in the morning and can't go in looking like the dog's dinner. The instructor's really cute and I think he's single, too. Night, girls! *(Exits side stairs.)*
JINX. Well, I've got a makeover at nine. *(Carries empty glasses to*

the bar.)
RANDA. Let me know if you can work me in tomorrow afternoon.
MARLAYFAYE. *(Chuckles.)* You know what really tickles me? Just when that kid's close to bein' *out* of diapers, his daddy's gonna be close to being *in* 'em. Hey, maybe they can get a family discount. *(Laughter.)*
RANDA. Well, congratulations again, Marlafaye. I never would've —
(Suddenly there's the sound of Dot falling, she cries out, then groans. Marla-faye sprints for the stairs, looks down.)
MARLAFAYE. *(To the others as she races out the side stairs.)* Dot fell! It's bad! Call 9-1-1! *(Verandah lights fade as Marlafaye and Jinx race down side stairs, Randa runs into kitchen and downstage right pin spotlight comes up.)*

Scene 3

Six weeks later. A mid-tempo 1960s girl-group song plays. Dot steps into the light, wearing slightly tinted glasses and a robe, her left arm in a sling.

DOT. Ross was always fond of saying, "Never ask a question if you really don't want to know the answer." Kind of like when the preacher's wife asked the little girl, "And why are we quiet in church?" The little girl whispered, "So we don't wake anybody up." *(Laughs.)* So when I went to the specialist — well, three specialists, but who's counting — I knew the answer to my question wouldn't be a good one, but the phrase "going blind" was not one I'd counted on hearing. I couldn't have faced this on my own … and I am so lucky I don't have to. *(Rallies. Pleasant, no trace of self-pity.)* Heavens, I've been around quite a while, maybe I've just *seen* my share. I've started memorizing faces, studying maps, trying to remember images of all the things I don't want to forget. So, time for me to adapt and change. The girls even convinced me it would be more convenient to sell my house on Tybee Island and move into the heart of Savannah. So I did. Jinx found an adorable carriage house two blocks from Randa's place and the four of us finished moving me in just today. While the fresh paint fumes dissipate, we're celebrating with an old-fashioned slumber party at Randa's. Guess who's going to have a good time tonight? I *definitely* know the answer to *that* question. *(The pin spotlight fades to black as lights come up on the verandah. Distant thunder of a spring storm is heard. Marlafaye, in a worn terrycloth bathrobe, is sprawled on the sofa. Jinx, in a sexy robe, collapsed in an armchair, her feet on the coffee table. Dot turns, walks into the light.)* I am absolutely in awe of you girls. You did the work of seven men this week! I've moved a few times in my life, but it *never* went this well.

JINX.   *(Unusually subdued.)* Listen, I'm a pro at moving. My philosophy is get it done fast and eliminate as much agony as possible.

MARLAFAYE.   Which is how *I'd* describe *sex after fifty.* *(Laughter. Randa, dressed in a frilly robe, slippers, enters from the kitchen with a tray of mugs.)*

RANDA.   Hot chocolate for everyone. Nothing but cocoa, milk, and sugar.

MARLAFAYE.   *(Takes a mug, stares at it.)* Huh. Okay, *missionaries* might enjoy your cocoa … *(Pulls a bottle from her purse.)* But *I'm* puttin' Kahlúa in mine.

JINX.   If you ever want to get rid of that magic purse, I'll take it. Hit me. *(Takes a mug, holds it out to Marlafaye.)*

DOT.   Me, too.

RANDA.   What the heck. *(Holds out her mug.)*

MARLAFAYE.   Now, that's more like it! *(Pours a splash in every mug, sits. They sip, relax.)* Yeah, we did a fine job on that house of yours, Dottie.

JINX.   I'm glad you wanted my sister's oval mirror. It looks great in your new entry.

DOT.   I'll treasure it. Oh, I wish I had known Toni.

JINX.   *(Wistful.)* Yeah, she was a helluva gal. *(Beat.)* I … uh, need a second. Be right back. *(Exits into kitchen. The others share a concerned look.)*

RANDA.   Poor Jinx. It's been weeks now and she's still having such a hard time with this.

MARLAFAYE.   We've gotta figure out what else we can do to help her through it.

DOT.   The timing couldn't have been worse. Jinx insisted she take me to that last specialist right after the funeral. I think my diagnosis hit her about as hard as it hit me.

MARLAFAYE.   Maybe since she can't do anything about *that* explains why she's worked nonstop to get you situated in the carriage house.

RANDA. Well, she pulled off a minor miracle finding it. And one of the things I really like about your new place, Dot, is that it's all on one level.

DOT. Me, too! Thank goodness there are no stairs. I wouldn't want a replay of *this. (Holds up her sprained arm.)* You know, I'd love to get a pet, but I'm allergic to dogs. Hey, anyone ever heard of a seeing-eye *cat? (Laughs.)*

MARLAFAYE. Don't even go there, Dottie. We're not givin' up on you yet.

DOT. Well, if you won't, I won't. *(Distant thunder.)* Don't you just love the sound of thunder? It's perfect for a slumber party. Of course I'm just guessing, I can't remember the last one I ever went to.

RANDA. Oh, I can. Freshman year in college. We raided the vending machines and ate Cheetos 'til we made ourselves sick and talked about boys 'til the sun came up.

MARLAFAYE. Then I say let's keep that tradition rollin'. I didn't want to tell y'all about this in case it went hellward, but I've actually had a date with someone I've never been married to. Dottie, it was Enrique, your EMT guy from the salsa dance.

RANDA. You sly thing!

MARLAFAYE. I ran into him at the Forsyth Farmers' Market. His squad had a fundraisin' booth and he saw me over at the Girl Scout cookie stand. We got to talkin' and he asked me out. *(Leans in.)* And you were so right, Dottie. The man does give *really* good mouth-to-mouth. *(The others cheer.)*

RANDA. Cookies! I picked up some Do-si-dos a couple of days ago. I'll go get them. *(Jumps up, hurries into the kitchen.)*

MARLAFAYE. Oh, good. That's my favorite kind of — *(Quickly, conspiratorial, to Dot.)* Have you noticed that Randa hasn't said a word all day about her brother?

DOT. Well, Alden disgraced himself, ended his political career before it started, and shamed his family in the process. I wouldn't talk about it either.

MARLAFAYE. But an affair with a senator's wife — with *explicit pictures*?! After the horrible way they've treated Randa all her life, I'd say the Covington Family put their money on the wrong — *(She stops abruptly as Randa enters from the kitchen door with a plate of cookies. Silence.)*

RANDA. You two have never been this quiet since the day I met you. Okay, I know what you're talking about, so let's cut to the

chase. I'm very sorry Alden made the choice that's ended what, no doubt, would've been a brilliant career. But there's no going back now. I wish him no further harm and that's that. *(Sets cookies on coffee table.)* I also wish I hadn't forgotten the napkins. *(Hurries into kitchen. Marlafaye and Dot grab a cookie.)*
MARLAFAYE. Well, hats off to Randa for takin' the high road.
DOT. You know, a lesser woman would celebrate her pompous brother's downfall. *(Unseen, Randa boogies in from the kitchen behind them with napkins, does a wild, silent victory dance — her revenge.)*
MARLAFAYE. Yeah, I'd gloat and rub his nose in it. Guess Randa's got more class than us. *(Randa dances toward them, stops, composes herself.)*
RANDA. Napkins, everyone. *(More thunder as Jinx enters from kitchen.)*
JINX. That thunder's getting closer. We may have to move inside.
MARLAFAYE. Hold your horses. There's somethin' I'd like to bring up. Jinx, you said if we thought our lives hadn't improved after followin' your advice we wouldn't pay. Well, it's been six months now, so I propose the three of us keep our end of the bargain. Time to cash in, Jenkins.
DOT. I second the motion!
JINX. No, I … I can't accept that.
RANDA. Why not? We did agree to it. You can use the money to start your new life-coaching business.
JINX. Look, maybe I had a few good ideas, but we sort of did it all together. Let's just call it even. I'm not going to take your money.
MARLAFAYE. *(Gasps.) "I'm not going to take your money?!"* One of the holy trinity of statements you never hear a true Southerner make, along with *"I'll have grapefruit instead of the biscuits"* and *"Elvis who?"*
DOT. Jinx, you've earned it. Look at us — we've all restarted our lives, got some wind in our sails, and we're having a ball.
JINX. It's okay, really. I'll just gouge my *next* clients … *(Turns. Quietly.)* Wherever that might be. *(Beat. Randa/Marlafaye/Dot exchange a look.)*
MARLAFAYE. Hold on! What did you just say?
RANDA. *Wherever that might be?* What're you talking about?
JINX. My sister didn't really have an estate for me to settle, so that's all finished, it's over. Everyone here's doing great and … well, maybe it's just time for me to move on. *(Off their stunned looks.)* And honestly, I'm not sure I can really look someone in the eye and tell them I know what's best for them. Maybe I need to rethink this whole life-coach thing. I mean, I'm as lost as I've ever been. Why should anyone listen to me?

DOT. So … you're leaving? Why?
JINX. Because … because —
RANDA. *(Gently.)* Because it's what you always do? *(It hangs in the air. Lights crossfade to black, downstage right pin spotlight comes up. Jinx walks into the light.)*
JINX. In truth, my sister left long before she died, but she was … *here.* I thought I was ready, I could handle the loss but now … she's gone and because of that, *nothing's* really the same. There's no one left who wants only the best for me. It hit me last week when I ran out to grab some lunch at a diner. I watched the waitress help an ancient fellow get himself and his walker to a table. She tucked a napkin into his collar and leaned down to help him figure out what he wanted for lunch. When she brought my order, I asked if he was her father. She said, "No. Poor old man is all alone. If he didn't eat here, I doubt he'd eat at all." She told me he shows up every day, by himself, and she wondered how that could be. She asked, "He's *got* to have someone. Where are they? Why aren't they here for him?" *(Simply, non-emotional.)* I can't get that out of my head, and I keep asking myself, "Who'll be there for me?" *(Beat. In the dark, Randa, Dot, and Marlafaye rise, cross downstage behind Jinx and stand just outside her light. Jinx continues to look out front as the others speak to her.)*
RANDA. We will. We're not going anywhere.
DOT. And you shouldn't either. You've pushed us to try new things to help rebuild our confidence. Maybe it's time you try that, too.
MARLAFAYE. Yeah. Stay in one place, find out what it feels like to finally put down roots.
DOT. You said maybe you move so much because you're looking for *that wonderful thing.* Well … what if you've found it? *(Beat. Dot, Marlafaye, and Randa exit stage left, Jinx turns her head slightly to watch them leave.)*
JINX. *(Turns out front again.)* If asked to describe it, I'd say Savannah is a city of Spanish moss, magnolias, legendary Southern charm and — to my surprise — three people who care about me. I came here to say goodbye to the last of my family and in the process I found another one … a family of friends. So … the students became the teacher — hey, maybe I did better than I thought. And now I finally realize … I don't have to run anymore … *(Smiles.)* I'm home. *(Pin spotlight fades to black.)*

Scene 4

One month later. Up-tempo, lively French accordion music comes up. A new pin spotlight comes up extreme downstage center. Randa, in slacks and a French-style striped pullover top and neck scarf, enters stage left, walks into the light with a champagne flute, gazes out, smiles with satisfaction.

RANDA. I admit I was a little nervous when we checked our bags for the flight. I asked the surly ticket agent why there was mistletoe hanging over the conveyor belt. She said, "So you can kiss your suitcase goodbye." *(Then.)* But we made it. It's hard to believe we're really here! I thought right now was the perfect time — we have so much to celebrate. For example, my very happy client gave me an unexpected bonus for finishing my preliminary design of his building. So, it was only logical for me to treat all four of us to a fabulous trip. *(Marlafaye enters stage left in trousers, t-shirt with "Paris or Bust" on it, carries a champagne flute and a baguette.) Another* baguette?
MARLAFAYE. *Oui, Madame.* On the plane I was readin' my *AARP* and do you know they have found out that women who carry a little extra weight tend to live longer than the men who call it to their attention?
RANDA. Really? Give me some of that. *(Pulls off a piece. Dot enters in tinted glasses, a skirt, top, binoculars around her neck, and a beret. She carries a bottle of champagne and a flute.)*
DOT. *(Ecstatic.)* You know, with these binoculars I can see the Eiffel Tower from my bedroom window! *C'est magnifique!* The whole trip is!
RANDA. Well, I just thought anyone who spent thirty years teaching high-school French in Oklahoma deserved to see more than Paris, Texas.
MARLAFAYE. *(Scolds, playful.)* Hey, now! Watch yourself! *(Jinx enters from stage left in slacks, a black turtleneck, carries a champagne flute, a collapsed selfie stick, camera attached.)*
JINX. How did you find this hotel? It's got the absolute best views!
RANDA. *(Gazes happily into the distance.)* Doesn't it?! Over there's the Seine and way over there, that hill, it's Montmartre.
JINX. Yeah, yeah, that's nice, too. What *I'm* talking about are all

50

those attractive Frenchmen everywhere you look! *(Dot quickly hands champagne to Marlafaye, looks through her binoculars.)*
DOT. Really, where? *(Searches the street below.)* Ooh, la la! *(Marlafaye fills each glass.)*
MARLAFAYE. Wow. Sippin' French champagne on a balcony in Paris, France. For a bunch of women over forty, we have got it goin' on! Never in my life did I dream I'd do this. Well, I did dream it once, but it involved a team of naked soccer players … so, it wasn't like this at all, really.
DOT. Oh, I'd love to hear more about that dream later.
JINX. Okay, we all would, but first, let's have a toast. I'll start —
RANDA. *(Teases.)* Always the coach.
JINX. What would we do if we hadn't met each other? *(Raises her flute.)* Here's to Paris! *(The others raise their flutes.)*
MARLAFAYE. And to Randa for gettin' us here!
DOT. And to finally seeing the Mona Lisa! *And* to knowing life is better when you have someone to talk to, laugh with, and share a glass with every now and then!
RANDA. And here's to believing it's never too late to make new old friends! *(They clink their flutes, sip. Jinx, Marlafaye, and Dot turn their backs to the audience and arrange themselves for a photo, Jinx extends selfie stick as Randa turns to the audience.)* I mean, it's only logical. Right? *(Smiles, turns her back to the audience, gets into place with the others. Jinx holds up the camera on the selfie stick.)*
RANDA/JINX/MARLAFAYE/DOT. Fromaaaage! *(FLASH of a camera! Up-tempo music comes up full. Blackout.)*

End of Play

PROPERTY LIST

Yoga mat
Water bottle
Large terrycloth rag doll
Gym bag
Purses
Shopping bag
Silver candlestick
Bouquet
4 library books
Food container
Large chunk of cheese
Plate of cookies
Oven mitts
Cookie sheet
Napkins
Baguette
Bill cap
Pillow
Small box with brooch and note
Bottle of nail polish
Blouse
Spray can
Sling
Binoculars
Selfie stick
Jug
Glasses for drinks, including wine glasses, cordial glasses, mugs,
        and flutes.
Bottles of alcohol, including wine, champagne, Kahlúa, Madeira,
        and bourbon

SOUND EFFECTS

Ding of oven buzzer

Note on Songs/Recordings, Images, or Other Production Design Elements

Be advised that Dramatists Play Service, Inc., neither holds the rights to nor grants permission to use any songs, recordings, images, or other design elements mentioned in the play. Jones Hope Wooten do not use copyrighted material in their plays. Any songs written into Jones Hope Wooten plays must be performed exactly as written, including but not limited to the indicated melody and the staging of such songs. No other songs, recordings, or production elements may be incorporated or substituted for specific elements written into the play.

If any copyrighted material is used in a production of a Jones Hope Wooten play, including but not limited to pre-show music, it is the responsibility of the producing theater/organization to obtain permission of the copyright owner(s) for any such use. Additional royalty fees may apply for the right to use copyrighted materials. Dramatists Play Service, Inc., does not assist in clearing rights to materials not specifically written into acting editions. DPS cannot advise as to whether or not a song/arrangement/recording, image, or other design element is in the public domain.

www.ingramcontent.com/pod-product-compliance
Lightning Source LLC
Chambersburg PA
CBHW061058050726
47592CB00004B/1734